Praise for the writings of Daniela Gioseffi

"One of the finest poets around . . . Her work overflows with poetic vision. Nothing is ever pretentious or done for effect."
        Nona Balakian, NBCC, *The New York Times*

"Visionary and powerful. Tremendous vitality. A gifted and graceful writer."
        Galway Kinnell, Pulitzer Prize,
        National Book Award winning poet

"Gioseffi's work is brilliant, compassionate, and timely—a pleasure to spend time with."
        D. Nurkse, poet, *Burnt Island*,
        NEA and NYSCA winner

"Startlingly fresh. Animated. Voluptuous. Mythopoeic."
        Mary Pradt, *Library Journal*

"A voice as true as a bird's or springtime . . . authenticity and sensitivity. She writes out of necessity and nothing is artificial . . ."
        Nina Cassian, Award Winning W.W. Norton poet

"In the shadow of world violence, and environmental devastation, she calls for the redeeming power of love: erotic love, mother love, community love . . ."
        Donna Masini, Director, Creative Writing, Hunter College.

"Gioseffi's writing is appealing . . . Engaging, filled with energy, . . . irresistible."
        Larry McMurty, *The Washington Post*

"I am grateful for your strong voice . . ."
        Marisa Frasca, Bordighera Press

"Your writing is beautiful as your mind . . ."
        Alicia Ostriker, Poet Laureate NYS,
        Academy of American Poets Board

VIA Folios 186

Also by Daniela Gioseffi

Waging Beauty as the Polar Bear Dreams of Ice: Poems

Me Too; Anch'io: Italian American Women's Writings, edited by Daniela Gioseffi

Pioneering Italian American Culture: Escaping La Vita della Cucina, edited by Daniela Gioseffi and Angelina Oberdan

The Story of Emily Dickinson's Master, Wild Nights! Wild Nights!

Blood Autumn/Autunno di sangue: Poems New and Selected, bilingual edition

Women on War: An International Anthology of Writings from Antiquity to the Present, edited by Daniela Gioseffi

Symbiosis: Poems

In Bed With the Exotic Enemy: Stories and Novella

Word Wounds and Water Flowers: Poems

Dust Disappears: Poems of Carilda Oliver Labra, translated by Daniela Gioseffi, with a foreword by Gregory Rabassa.

Wildlife of Northwest New Jersey: An Introductory Guide to Flora and Fauna of the Skylands Region, with illustrations by Pamela Mading

On Prejudice: A Global Perspective, edited and introduction by Daniela Gioseffi

Women on War: Essential Voices for the Nuclear Age, edited and introduction by Daniela Gioseffi

Earth Dancing, Mother Nature's Oldest Rite

Eggs in the Lake: Poems with foreword by John Logan

The Great American Belly Dance

The Brooklyn Bridge Poetry Walk, edited by Daniela Gioseffi

Stardust Lives in Us

Published by Bordighera Press, an imprint of the John D. Calandra Italian American Institute of Queens College, The City University of New York.

25 West 43rd Street, 17th Floor, New York, NY 10036

All rights reserved. Parts of this book may be reprinted only by written permission from the publisher, and may not be reproduced for publication in media of any kind, except in quotations for the purposes of literary reviews.

Library of Congress Control Number: 2025942489

Cover image from TyliJura, Pixabay

Ellery J. Sampson selected the cover image and designed a first draft of the cover.

© 2025, Daniela Gioseffi

VIA Folios 186
ISBN 978-1-59954-241-6

STARDUST LIVES IN US

Daniela Gioseffi

BORDIGHERA PRESS

Dedicated to my daughter Thea, and grandsons Ellery and Keir, to remind them that I believe in their future and hope for their wellbeing, and do what I can to save and respect *Mother Earth,* our planet home.

In memory of my Italian immigrant father, Daniel Donato Gioseffi who taught me tenacity and who first read poetry to me, and in memory of my mother Josephine B. Gioseffi who taught me persistence and nature's beauty.

I am also profoundly grateful to my literary executrix Angelina Oberdan Brooks for all her work through the years.

Table of Contents

I. Mother Earth and Her Breathing Trees

One Small Blue Dot	13
The Trees Are Warning Us	15
Amber Waves of Dying Grain	17
Fragility	18
21st Century Ironies	22
Sixth Extinction?	24
The Plan	28
Yes, to the Trees	30
After Our Fall from Eden, God Speaks?	32
Mother Earth, You're a City of Lilies and Apple Trees	34
Earth offers ecstasy,	36
Our Peaceable Longing	39
Mother Earth, Gaia	40
Dark Matter Illuminates and Beguiles	41
Carbon Summer or Nuclear Winter	43
Cataclysmic Carousel of Greed	45
Chant for Sioux Water Protectors of Standing Rock	47

II. Longings

Beyond the East Gate	51
Erotic Furies in the News	53
The weighty everlasting wait of waiting women,	55
For the Venus of Willendorf	57
The Origins of Milk	58
To Lost and Found Love	61
The Art of Loneliness	63
Some Slippery Afternoon	65
Evening Hours Before Sleep	67
Rejection Makes Wings with Each Little Death It Offers	69
Peopled with the Dead	71
Is there survivor's guilt after the pandemic	72
Spring has come again!	74

As When Some Silenced Singer Hears Her Aria	75
Imagine all the pounding hearts	76

III. Stardust Lives in Us

The Blue Whale	81
When History's Truth Is Amazing Grace	83
Yes, to Life	85
The trees are dying	87
Oh Gaia, Dear Mother	89
Turning into Light	90
A Dreaming Child Comes to Me in My Dream	92
Liberty and Justice	93
We're Stardust and Water	95
Big-hearted, Witty and Wide-Eyed	98

Acknowledgements	101
About the Author	105

I.
MOTHER EARTH
AND HER BREATHING TREES

We are called to assist the Earth to heal her wounds, and, in the process, heal our own—indeed to embrace the whole of creation in all its diversity, beauty and wonder.

Wangari Maathai of Kenya

The poet now wants to talk with the trees.

Jules Renard

Our Small Blue Dot

for Carl Sagan

Looking back from space at our small blue dot
with thin veil of atmosphere, giving all breath
and language from lungs exhaling through larynx,
to make music and words of love,
sculpted by our dancing tongues.
We see we breathe with fruitful trees,
giving oxygen to children to live after us,
to hear our music, see our art,
read our poetry's philosophies —
monstrous wars, are petty, pitiable,
while we're one small breathing planet of life—
trees, birds and song.
We're a rainbow of Earthlings
threatened to death
by our common enemies,
toxins from oil, gas, coal,
death dug up from bowels of Earth,
nuclear radiation pouring back on us,
uniting us as one endangered species.
That Love is all there is,
Is all we know of love, said Emily Dickinson.
 Love, that soothing biting emotion,
 keeps the human race alive as it struggles
against hate, jealousy, envy's bulging eyes.

Mammalian mother's love of the nursing child
is the root of love, and where love begins,
as the *light* in their comingled gaze.

Women's breasts are the origin of milk
and the root of love, *not only sex symbols,*
but the very connection of human life
to Earth's photosynthesizing trees,
and atmospheric balance.

The suckling child
gazing into the mother's eyes
begins all mutual human love.

The Trees Are Warning Us

talking under earth with each other
on a sultry summer day,
sharing deeply. Science says
trees are social beings. Trees do what we do,
when we're kind: trade ideas
about health, weather and food.

Trees support birds, insects, us.
Trees live sane lives and generate good *karma*.
Glance upward while standing under plush trees
and sense the true green cathedrals of Earth.
They're scared, warning each other of
trouble. It will take a congregation of loving
spirits to save them and us and our
beloved young who live by their grace.
Listen to the trees as the living, breathing,
companions of life on Earth creating
atmospheric balance, photosynthesizing
food for mammalian breasts
as the first link in the food chain
that nourishes us.

Listen! The trees are warning us:
Flying, swimming, and walking creatures
are missing in action! The casualty list
keeps growing with dying elephants, bears, whales
shorebirds, bees and food crops.
More than half the world's wild life now extinct.
Public protests against climate catastrophe
are weakened by pandemics and wars
as white cedars die in Jersey's Pine Barrens

and climate fires destroy homes in California
as almond tree farms and drinking water
dry up in thirsty Atlanta, Georgia,
and fish swim in drowning Miami streets.

Unlike *karma* we're producing—
through competitive *turbo*-capitalist greed,
Earth sculpts itself with water, wind, quaking
and drying as *climate* justice joins with *social* justice
to say that trees give life teaches us love.

Amber Waves of Dying Grain

We live in the shadows of immense hands
like death that will take our sex away.

Bridal days and wedding nights of grace and youth
and doors opening in women.

Music is a child of the grass
and teaches us the cost of frostbite.

We can't separate the misunderstandings
or wash dishes in the music box.

We talk and spend the word on our burning hands.
A cinder of a joke catches in our throat.

We laugh to hold onto the hurrying waters.
A fern is a fan that resembles a rainbow.

Clay is prerogative;
eyes are derivative.

The last ghosts of Indians are asking for water
in the amber waves of dying grain.

Fragility

        after reading astrophysicist Neil DeGrasse Tyson

A mere sixty million years ago,
less than 2% of Earth's past,
a ten-trillion-ton asteroid
hit what's now
the Yucatan Peninsula
and obliterated more than 70%
of Earth's flora and fauna—
      and all the huge dinosaurs,
      reptiles with huge bodies
      and small brains.

That disaster allowed mammals
      to fill the vacancy
          left by large cold-blooded lizards.

One big-brained species of those mammalian
      ancestors, apes, became us,
      with enough intelligence
      to invent tools and mathematical equations
      like $E=MC^2$
      energy as matter
      and matter as energy,

and to deduce the universe evolved
from a teeny tiny *nano*-particle that exploded
            with a *Big Bang*
      forming particles that after
      billions of years
      collected into life.

But, no one knows
>   what happened before that *Big Bang*
>   or how that *nano*-particle got there.

That's why we invented God
>   and why he's never been entirely knocked off
>   his heavenly throne as prime mover.

But, what if the universe was always there
>   in sempiternity? What if
>   there is a multi-universe
>   that continually gives birth
>   to other universes?

What if the universe popped
>   into existence from nothing,
>   not even the first hydrogen molecule?
>   What if we are mere computer simulations?
>   rendered for the entertainment of a great
>   super-entity of species?

Those who believe
>   they are ignorant of nothing
>   have never looked for
>   the boundaries between what's known
>   and unknown.

Yet what we do know is that every atom
>   of our bodies is traceable back to that
>   big explosion, *a Big Bang* of stardust
>   from thermo-nuclear furnaces within stars
>   that exploded more than 14 billion years ago.

We are stardust brought to life,
>   empowered to figure out

       who and what we are
       and where we can go
       we've only just begun to know.

Meantime people kill and get killed
       in the name of someone else's God
       and some kill because they are hungry,
       and some kill because they are greedy,
       and some kill because they love
       and some kill because they think they love.

We do not just live in the universe.
       The universe lives in us.

There are more stars in the universe
       than words and sound ever uttered
       by all the humans who ever lived
       and when we breathe,
       we breath the same molecules
       and drink the same water
       that passed through Socrates or Joan of Arc,
       Napoleon, Madame Curie, Lincoln or Beethoven.
       {Continue with stanza break->

There are more stars in the universe
       than grains of sand on any beach;
       more stars have exploded and died
       then seconds have passed since
       Earth formed,

and we still do not know who
       or what we are
       and where we are going,
       though we're becoming smart enough
       to kill ourselves
       by destroying our only planet home

upon which we've traveled
4.6 billion trips around the sun
since we began.

21st Century Ironies

Will pet lovers accuse me
of *a guilt trip?*

Everyone loves dogs. They're sometimes nicer
than people. But, I see dogs barking at each other
as they pass on leashes of masters
who let them sniff each other's rears, saying "Hello,
who are you; what did you have for dinner?"
to each other's back ends.

I think of tons of dog poop in city garbage trucks
scooped into plastic bags polluting landfills and water.
Monumental amounts of plastics poisoning
drinking water with micro-bits of polymers
that adhere to toxic chemicals. Micro-plastics
now in our most pristine water sources
and in our veins and brains causing illness!

I watch the many dogs owned by the lonely
who walk the streets and meet to play in parks.
And I think of all starving children, yes,
starving children, even in inner cities
of rich America, left unfed.

I walk down huge isles of pet foods, treats, and toys
in the big supermarkets displaying monumental
amounts of brightly colored packages and cans,
and all the pet store chains from *Petco* to *PetSmart,*
everywhere that sell the same, and am I wrong to cringe
at the photos of starving Yemeni, Bangladeshi,

African, Palestinian, Ukrainian . . . and American,
 American children starving?

Sixth Extinction?

> after reading Elizabeth Korbert,
> Pulitzer Prize winning biologist

Along with all sumptuous fruits,
flowers fully bloomed,
we're dooming ourselves,
We're dropping our gorgeous petals
in putrid oil slime, *fossils of dead things*
burned into our skies, fouling our lungs
in a world energized by death
pumped up from Earth's bowels.

After two-hundred thousand years
on our home, billions of years
older than us we're able
to name all things and each other
and claim all as our own.

Our opposing thumbs and big brains
didn't make us huge as dinosaurs
or elephants, or speedy and agile as lions,
tigers, cheetahs, crocodiles,
but *inventive, adaptive*
to varied regions of our planet home.

We built bridges, boats, trains, cars, planes,
crossed rivers, oceans, mountains,
deserts, conquered all predators,
even *ourselves*, with pillaging wars.

All wildlife became our prey to hunt
and kill, giant mammals to tiny

insects, bacteria, viruses.
Big animals larger than us
wiped out!

We've battled other species
for thousands of years,
and reproduced at a rate overwhelming
our food and water supply.
We dominate all species
with our weapons beyond belief.
Like *King Midas's Touch* of greed
destroys all
as powerful rich men, oligarchs,
believe, *not love*,
but all that glitters *is* gold.

In a mere century our population doubled
and doubled again and again. Vast forests
maintaining atmospheric balance,
our very breath,
were chopped to dust, clear cut
to build and furnish houses.

We've flown around the globe
envying wings and spewing jet fumes,
we dominate birds, bees, and butterflies
to the point of killing pollinators
of our food, fruits and vegetables.

Frogs who sang billions of years before us
have stopped singing and will soon no longer
grace our ponds, or tables with their legs
almondine, as almond trees run out of water.

We've carried organisms from continent
to continent and changed our biosphere

to threaten our lives and all living things.
Fearful of mixing genes of varied skin tones,
we lag behind rats who've fortified
their immunity with inter-breeding.

With prejudice based on skin color.
we've kept from strengthening
our genes, holding them hostage
in factious racial and religious wars.

Now, biologists believe only giant rats
will survive our extinction.

We're the *paragon of animals*
with complex languages and highly technical
communications, and subtle emotions
from love and empathy to hate,
sadness and ecstatic elation.

We've dug up subterranean reserves of
dead forests and fossilized animals from the putrid
guts of Mother Earth to fuel our technocratic
civilization with coal, oil, and gas, burning
them enough to choke ourselves into oblivion
with industrial waste and artificial intelligence.

Disaster happened before without us
when a meteorite bombed dinosaurs to death, but,
irony of ironies, we discovered
Five Big Extinctions, just as we're about
to kill ourselves in a self-made Sixth!

Only as late as the 19th century
did we learn of the demise of dinosaurs
and mammoths, as we found remains of huge teeth,
tusks and bones. In winter 2017,

we found a six-foot tall penguin skeleton
in Greenland where *auks* were driven
to death by mid-19th century hunters.

Natural Selection ruled our ideas of
Survival of Fittest, until a woman biologist,
Lynn Margulis, once astrophysicist Carl Sagan's wife,
discovered *symbiosis* and taught us
that *cooperation* is as important as *competition*
in survival of our species. She argued that
"Natural selection eliminates and maintains,
but it doesn't create."

She discovered *symbiosis* as the major driver
of evolutionary change, not only *natural selection*,
not just "survival of the fittest" but *symbiotic cooperation*
has made our lives possible
and built our civilization.

The earliest families were *women*,
in the manner of elephant and deer herds.
While men roamed, hunted,
grabbed women when they could
to force procreation.

Our *Anthropocene Age*
asks a question to *all of us:*.
To be, or not to be?
That is the question!

The Plan

> *God is the love all of nature creates in us,*
> *and greed for things is killing this beautiful life.*
> Donato Gioseffi (1905-1981) philosopher, Puglia, Italia

The plan was for butterflies,
bees and bats to suck among flowers,
gathering sweetness to live
as they carried pollen, seed to ova,
to bring fruit from need.

The plan was for waters
to run freshly through
wetland deltas, filtering streams
along their way from mountain tops
quenching thirst running clear
rivers to the sea bringing life to the lips of children,
blossoming from the need for love
from parents, two different animals united
into a new being, ecstatic with rebirth.

The plan was for forests to clean the air
for children's breath in symbiotic balance
using carbon dioxide expelled from animals
to give forth oxygen,
to photosynthesize food from need,
making green leaves that leaf and leaf again
to feed women's breasts, not mere objects of sex,
but factories of milk, first link
in the food chain for children's mouths
to suckle milk from leaves of grass
come from fertile mud for need.
But sheer greed for things of plastic,

polymers from petroleum:
acrylic, polyester, biogenetics,
nuclear radiation, poisons,
greed for too much meat full of steroids,
land laid waste grazing cattle,
carcinogens, plutonium, filth and waste,
killed the plan slowly, bit
by bit, until the water trickled
with foul waste of industries' mistakes
and what was needed food, water, breath
was suffocated to a barren death.

Bats, bees and butterflies
ceased to buzz around flowers
bearing fruit from their sexual union
and children had no food.
Forests chopped to dust
gave forth no oxygen
or photosynthesis
or atmospheric balance
as fluorocarbons and fuel emissions
opened holes in the ozone
and burned the earth
to a carbon crisp,
while love,
which is God itself,
no longer breathed
in the eyes of children,
but was silenced from its song
and art, books, poems,
had no feelings to speak
as all seed,
through "market engineering,"
was lost
to greed.

Yes, to the Trees

Trees are the oldest living beings on Earth;
80,000-year-old groves of Quick Aspens,
13,000-year-old Eucalyptus Trees,
3,000-year-old ancient redwoods,
Giant Sequoias threatened by climate wildfires.
Since our beginnings, trees have given us life
And now we're polluting life with decayed life's
sludge, oil, death dug up to kill us. What irony!

We need to tell the world how to treat life,
because greed has put all life in deep trouble.
We're committing *Ecocide* by burning
Earth's dead matter, oil of rotted dinosaurs,
tar, sludge from ancient vegetation underground,
dirty energy burned, killing the living trees and us.
We can broadcast love of trees who nourish
us with breath, food, shelter, shade
Can we live with faith fierce enough
to live in peace with tranquil trees,
and love our children as our life hereafter?

Since the dawn of time, trees
have been our silent companions;
they bear steadfast witness to our earthly lives
while reaching up to heaven prayerfully.

We ask them for answers and they reply
with comforting green glory from the sun,
as they recycle water to exchange
life giving breath with us.
Without their companionship there is no life,

and they are burning up in wars and wildfires.
I walk every morning
under the trees who talk to me of love,
and how we are preparing to leave life
sight, sound, smell to the children, and I ask
are we planting and replanting,
are we letting old forests live
to give new life for our children?
Are we saying *yes* to the trees?

After Our Fall from Eden, God Speaks?

after reading GENESIS

Their fall is all my doing, because I
put the *Tree of Knowledge* in The Garden
to tempt my children, Adam of the Earth,
and his lover, Eve of the Living. I did not want
Adam to be as lonely as I was, so utterly alone
before I made them to be beloved beholders
of my bounteous creation.

Am I jealous that the snake took away
Eve's love of me? He seduced my woman,
with a mind of her own, and made her fall
from my benevolent grace. Where did
that serpent come from? Was he created
out of my own insecure ego?

To test my children's love of me,
did the snake of my own curiosity
creep out of my insecurity
to beguile and seduce my children,
and make them fall from the Paradise
I made for them? They fear my power now,
more than they love me. They hide
in order that I discover them, call them
by name, and take pity on them.
They gave themselves the artifice
of fig leaves to cover their shame
which they did not have until they ate
of my apple from my *Tree of Knowledge*.
I've sent them forth out of my *Eden*.
Let me observe and see if they will find

their way back to my *Paradise*.
I've taken pity on them, given them animal
skins, fruits of my vegetation, dominion over all,
and sent them forth, *Paragon* of all my creation
to live in a *Domain of Pleasure, Death and Sorrow.*

I will be unbearably lonely again
if *Adam of the Earth* kills himself,
with greedy consumerism and war and takes
Eve of the Living, and all their children,
with him into eternal oblivion.

Mother Earth, You're a City of Lilies and Apple Trees

All creatures meet in your house of eyes, lips, kisses,
drafts of wine in the blessed wind, water and sun.
We live, Mother, under your dome of blue atmosphere
where our exhaled breath is communion, your house a bed
in a chamber of green. Oh, Mother Gaia, we come
from your round belly
to be blessed with feelings of wonder, joy, love,
the real gods that leap like gazelles in the eyes of children.
We can sleep in fragrant Chambers of Lavender,
and cling together against the threat of the death
of everything brought upon ourselves
with oil wars of greed, systemic pesticides in seeds,
a carbon dome that aggravates the Sun King
to overheat oceans of dying fish who swallow plastic!

All my words were for you, my lost beloved. All
for you, I'd make safe haven for children
who could have come from us— new
beings made of our bodies and minds joined, a child
come from our ancestors blended into one. I belong to you
and we belong to death as much as to life. If only love
were as strong as life, more than envy and greed,
we'd live in *Gaia's* Chamber of Fragrance, Our Mother,
Earth, a City of Lilies, Roses, Apples, Milk and Honey,
forever alive in those to come from us.

My great grief, beloved, is that I never found you
to have a child with you though the children I've had

are beloved. Let us help save all children
from the greed that makes misery, floods, hunger, famine.

Oh, Mother Earth, you could be a city of apple trees and lilies
if only wars were ended!

Earth offers ecstasy,

if we close our eyes and let our mind drift out
into the expanding universe past the distant stars
so many light years away imagination can't reach them.

Yet, they sparkle. We've invaded them with our telescopes
and know that the universe goes on beyond
and beyond them and us, so tiny, too briefly alive,
too transient to covet wealth or harbor hate for vulnerable
Earthlings like us on one small blue-green planet home
swirling together in darkness for a second in sempiternity,
as the universe flies out around us, endless space full of unknown
dark energy, pulling everything into it, as we're disappearing
aging, wrinkling with our delicate feelings
emoting inside our little flesh temples
from where we can reach out into an awesome mystery,
Gaia force of all nature, waters churning with winds,
melting glaciers, vast oceans rocking endlessly
from which we emerged crawling from waves onto shores.

To have ecstasy with Earth, let yourself feel how minuscule
you are in vast space, alive and breathing in the moment. Open
your mind to creation's awesome mysterious force
that brought all forth on this spinning globe of dancing blue
waters, frothy white waves, land masses of brown
and green from which we're all born of mud,

and now, we're making oceans rise by spewing
tons of poisonous carbon into the delicate veil
of our atmosphere, thin sphere of breath that fills
our lungs with life and exhales language. We are creators
of mythologies of Fallen Angels, Devils, Satan, Beelzebub:

Our own hellish symbols of greed rise in fires of heat
bringing all to the brink of extinction as glaciers melt away
releasing great clouds of methane from ocean floors to boil
the Earth beyond our endurance, so Devils of all mythologies
win over all legendary patriarchal gods: Zeus, Yahweh, Allah,
as greed for profits destroys all teachings of the prophets of love,
Moses, Jesus, Mohammed in whose name men wage wars,
to rape and kill women and children as the globe overheats
beyond endurance, destroying delicate compassion,
feelings of love that raise endorphins
into a realm of joy that dies with us as the world
economy collapses and all our books, music, poetry,
dancing, paintings, happiness, innocent babies,
actual angels of Earth, burn or drown floating away
with no memory of us, leaving not a trace in a
sixth extinction! See the books soaked and drifting
in the tides, museums flooded with rotting paintings,
computers fried, messaging ended, electrical grids
turned off, music silenced, Earth naked of life as it spins
floating toward Vega into the darkness of an expanding universe,
into nothingness, all flesh voided beyond feelings
as the devil of greed wins in *Revelations,* and we realize
too late that Paradise was actually
                                       here to be made…

Gaia force can be worshipped with eco-logic:
our sun warming us, photosynthesizing to feed
women's breasts, first link in the food chain that sustains us,
creating mammalian milk connecting us to Earth's bounty, forests
of food giving breath, breathing out oxygen as we among animals
breathe out carbon dioxide for their green lives.

The poetry of photosynthesizing trees, singing birds, flowers
of every hue, great blue heron, red cardinal, purple violet,
crimson rose, lavender orchid, yellow sunflower,
dancing crane, phenomenal humming bird of iridescent wings,

crawling ant, trumpeting, intelligent elephants
killed for their ivory tusks, giggling bonobo monkeys greeting with love,
chimpanzees arguing like us, rhinos with coveted horns, hippopotami
floating their huge hulks, swimming with crocodiles!
Glistening fish in fluorescent colors dying in acidifying oceans,
the multitudes of rainbow children who will suffer,
their eyes looking up to us with wondrous gaze,
truest angels of the universe needing us to save them, now.

Rise up for the eco-sphere of great rivers
now polluted and dying, mountains beheaded
for noxious coal, farmlands drying!

Let the wetlands naturalize! Let air, soil and waters breathe
free of poisons killing, bees and butterflies who live
to pollinate sweet fruits, vegetables! Turn off cancerous
plutonium bombs of Hell! Oh, this is how
          we have ecstasy with Earth!
Just open your heart to vast creation.

To have the thrill of ecstasy with Earth
we need only a loving heart
that beats through our blood.

Our Peaceable Longing

for Edward Hicks, artist of The Peaceable Kingdom

The kingdom we long for
could be as we dream of it daily
as distant bombs and guns fill the air
elsewhere with smoke, pain, and ruin.

Our longing continues
and the animals can only wait,
with the children for peaceful
humans to join them in the forest
where human and wild animal
converge to live unharmed by one another.

Why does the lion sit so full of wisdom,
ignoring the oxen who peers at him?

Why do the ram and bear rub noses together
as if in a kiss? Why do the children play
ignored by the tiger and lion, even
as one tweaks the nose of the leopard?

Far off from the innocence of animals and children
the merchants are bartering furs and oil with the natives,
while the lamb rests in stillness and the lion, leopard,
tiger are indifferent to their possible prey.

Animals of every kind keep patient vigil
while merchants haggle and we harbor
our peaceable longing as we wait
and long for and try
       for a peaceful kingdom.

Mother Earth, Gaia

We've seen Her from outer space,
one big blooming woman.
We're all born out of Her sapphire globe,
gleaming with frothy white waves and browns and greens
of forest and farmlands. When we saw Her
from outer space, life recognized *life*.
She emerged flying from the sun's explosion,
spun Herself into roundness to rotate endlessly,
journeying round the sun. Primal being without mouth, legs,
arms, or genitalia, she sails round the sun, spinning us
through days into sleep-filled nights. Her moon
creates tides on Her watery surface. Hospitable regions
of Her lands and seas birthed many organisms and, finally,
the ones with consciousness: we who issued from Her,
we individuals of Her global community, we– all of us–
Her children, dependent upon Her atmospheric balance
and photosynthesis fostering multitudinous varieties
of consumable vegetation. Spewing lava, molten glass
from sand, burning, acrid, smoking,
Gaia it seemed, had no future. Who would have thought
that from Her roundness so many beings would be born?
Who could have guessed that from Her flaming hot magma
forests, cities, songs, art, poetry, longings would be born?
Please come be Her celebrant with me, hope with me that our children,
born of Her womb, will live with Her breath, breathing with Her trees
in symbiotic balance, bathing in Her cleansed waters, tranquilly together,
Earthlings suckled by Her full-breasted bounty
of brown earth and blue-green waters.

Dark Matter Illuminates and Beguiles

> after reading Lisa Randall, Harvard cosmologist,
> author of *Dark Matter and the Dinosaurs*

Sixty-six million years ago, a tiny twitch caused
by an invisible cosmic force hurled a comet
three times the breadth of Manhattan
toward Earth at 700 times the speed of a freeway car.

The collision stirred the strongest earthquake known,
released energy a billion times that of an atomic bomb,
heating the atmosphere into an incandescent furnace
killing three-quarters of Earthly life. No creature bigger
than 55 pounds survived. Deaths of the dinosaurs
gave mammals dominance, and so we've evolved
to ponder the perplexities of the cosmos.

"Extinctions destroy life, but they also reset
the conditions for life's evolution." From dinosaurs
evolved the birds that sing to us mornings
and animate our skies. Meteorites deposited
the amino acids that became the seeds of our lives.

Rilke wrote: *The future enters into us in this way
in order to transform itself in us long before it happens.*
Parallel truths give our world complex richness in grand
schemes more wondrous than we imagine. The deadly comet
that birthed mammalian dominance took light years
to reach Earth and quake dinosaurs out of existence,
but their fate was sealed in a cosmic blink when dark matter
jolted the icy comet out of orbit.
Unknown in the physics of space
and biology of life bewilderment intertwined.

The gestational period of consequences can be immensely long,
and we've been heating our breathable atmosphere, a thin
veil around our planet home, for two hundred years. In our lifetime,
the human population has twice doubled, straining Earth's resources,
changing cosmic work billions of years in the making.

Our impact on our planet home is a slow-moving
                                      comet headed for doom.
But, there's a short time in which to avert its deadly course,
a catastrophe we've aimed at ourselves
with contagious consuming.

Carbon Summer or Nuclear Winter

Some say the world will end in fire
Some say in ice . . .
      Robert Frost

I look in my grandchild's eyes,
watch his small hands spin his toy globe
as Earth's fever rises. Glacial cliffs slide
into rising seas. Cities drown in flooding ports.
Climate refugees migrate upland to alien cultures
where religions clash in wars. Storms batter cities.
Forests cleared for greed rip species from the web of life.
Every day, millions of tons of brain-damaging poison
are dumped into the delicate shell of Earth's air
as if it's an endless sewer out there.
Reservoirs dry, cities burn in thirst.
Faltering farmers lose their living.
Pollinating bats, honeybees, butterflies and hummingbirds
die weakened by herbicides and pesticides.
Amphibians and birds diminish to extinction.
People of the Arctic and Pacific islands flee ancient lands.
Wildfires foul air and force thousands from burning homes.
Nuclear radiation spreads by tsunamis or earthquakes
as wars topple governments. Weapons dealers profit
as tanks and bombers guzzling oil.
Where lies collide with eco-logic,
battlefields bloom with blood.

I watch my grandson's small hands spin
his toy globe, and realize there could be
no eyes, no ears, no hands, no art, no song,
as our dusty planet, home to our dried tears

of love and laughter— lost in endless space,
could rotate frozen or burning in silent thirst.

Some say the world will end in carbon summer,
Some say in nuclear winter—
but from what I've seen of carbon fire,
nuclear winter ice is also great
and would suffice.

Cataclysmic Carousel of Greed

> *Turning and turning in the widening gyre*
> *The falcon cannot hear the falconer;*
> *Things fall apart; the center cannot hold....*
>   William Butler Yeats, "The Second Coming"

A cataclysmic carousel of greed
turns the world, spinning death high on the wing
turning faster and faster in *widening gyre.*

Cassandra rides weeping, yelling warnings
for the spinning children who ride with her,
rotating on Earth's breast, our only home
where our young could die of droughts,
thirst, floods, and hunger.

The children riding behind her cry:
No more killing; no more drilling!
Earth erupts, rumbling from killing
quaking, shaking from drilling.
Seismic blasting in the Arctic seas
deafens whales and dolphins, killing
murdering them and us.

Glaciers melt, oceans warm gaining weight,
shifting tectonic plates. Tsunamis surge
from acid seas, washing tons of dead fish ashore,
as Cassandra weeps Her dirge:
...what rough beast, its hour come round at last,
Slouches towards Bethlehem to be born?

Cassandra, gone insane, spins crying in pain:

No more drilling! No more killing!
A Trojan Horse gallops mad falconer astride,
yelling: "Make America great again! USA! USA—
 commanding his white armies, bellowing male pride.

Chant for Sioux Water Protectors of Standing Rock

Many have lived without love, but none without water.
         W.H. Auden

Oil is ancient fossilized death
putrefied life rotting for centuries
deep in the bowels of Earth.
Water is life. Oil is death!

Death was drilled from bowels of Earth,
spilled in oceans to foul water and kill
sea life on which we live.
Water is life. Oil is death!

Death was pumped from Earth's guts
and spewed into our children's breath
as asthma and lung disease.
Water is life. Oil is death!

"Black gold" was pulled from Earth's bowels
and dumped into skies as climate chaos:
super storms, earthquakes,
droughts, wildfires, floods.
Water is life. Oil is death!

A world powered by living Earth
can now be built
under shining sun
and stirring wind.
Water is life. Oil is death!
If political will is not strangled by greed,

strangled of breath, strangled to death,
it could be done. It can be done!

*Water is life returned by the sun,
driven by wind, driven by wind!*

II.
LONGINGS

*That love is all there is
Is all we know of love*

Emily Dickinson

*The rarer action is in virtue
than in vengeance*

Prospero, William Shakespeare, *The Tempest*

Beyond the East Gate

I listen to the voice of the cricket,
loud in the quiet night, warning me
not to mistake a hill for a mountain.

I need to be alone, in a private house
with doors that open only outward,
safe from strangers who smell of death,
where I can draft a universe under my eyelids
and let nothing invade it.

I want to sing a fugue
sounding like the genius of flowers
talking to leaves on their stems,
to have more concrete meaning
than even the dance of a child in my uterus.

I'm a lost and primitive priestess
wandering in a walled city of the wrong century.
I need to spend thirty years in the desert
before I will understand the sun,
thirty years at sea
to gather the blessing of salt and water.

In the back room of my skull
a secret dice game determines
the rites of my hands
before they touch flesh again.

I want to reach a peace I've never known,
to be an old woman who is very young,

a child who is a sage
come down from the mountain.

Erotic Furies in the News

Throughout history,
>men seem enveloped
>by sexual temptations,
>responsive to the incessant call
>of lustful desire.

Women more often look for a mate
>to make a home for family
>to feel loved in and safe.

Many men, perhaps most,
>are obsessed in a grip
>of carnal fervor
>facing arrays of ethical quandaries.

It's easy to imagine cave men
>bent on procreative urges
>with no forethought-- that driving
>biological itch, but what
>of civilized men?

Why do many modern tumescent men
>do what they do?

Step into the driven male mind,
>into the reality of pure urges,
>the obstinate pressures
>of hot desires intense as sheer lunacy,
>obsessions that needs to be understood
>to end wars wherein women's bodies
>are always part of power's booty—

        since the dawning of *homo sapiens*,
        since Aeschylus's *Suppliant Women*,
        since the *Rape of the Sabine Women*.
        abducted "Comfort Women" for Japan's Army,
        ongoing global trade in sexual slavery,
        Hollywood audition couches,

the constant rape of women in war,
            women's bodies the bounty
                      of male power.

The weighty everlasting wait of waiting women,

waiting for men to bring food from the hunt,
to return from war with smoking guns. Through centuries,
we bow our heads in supplication over soup pots
or grey washtubs and dream of romance rarely fulfilled
after we've given all to Father God
—commanding from on high; Yahweh or Zeus,
who say, "Wait for a good word from me!"
And so, we waited, and wait, tied by our love for children,
sons or daughters. We wait making homes for men.

If we go out after them, we're deemed aggressive,
bad, dirty, unseemly, whorish, unfeminine, so we wait,
empty vessels prepared for action in the kitchen or bed,
ready for whatever is poured into us, soups or sperm,
to simmer as we stir pots in anger, raging with our spoons,
ready for the attack, gonads poised, ready for travelling sperm,
waiting ova floating down to meet his spark,
waiting for life to come in us, waiting for peace to explode in us
waiting for love to fuse in us, counting on it, alone
with our children, all over the planet, we wait

for the fire bombs of angry erections or the erect bayonets
to come stabbing out of the jungle, wait for firm life to be sucked
into our bellies, waiting to be reborn with milky breasts,
life from flesh into flesh. On and on into and out of
our legs from which all come and go peeking beneath our skirts.

Mother Earth waiting for sun or rain to fall upon her belly,
seeds to be planted, with light or tears to come,

and we threaten with weeping cries, causing guilt,
longing to awaken from our wait, pacing, waiting
for moonbeams to shine through our torn veil of sky,
clouded mystery we are even to ourselves

as we come from our own bodies as men fear us
and love/hate us as their mothers, wanting
to be held, comforted, wanting to be free, always telling us
double messages of love me, let me go and be free but keep me, and so
we wait slowly dry out, naked arms once thin girl's
grown plump and tired, bodies soft tipped growing frost over our lips,
as we wait, slowly wrinkling in time, doomed to silence.

Fingers curl around our angers, as we wait, fires burning low,
as we wait, saying to ourselves, *ah, when I was young
he wanted me so, when I was young he chased me over the wet grass,
captured and put me in this place of waiting, for him to come
and fill me with life that arrives as death—*

we wait, a vessel among cups, sauce pans,
sinks, washtubs, bowls, dishes, vases, waiting
at the windows, widows' walks on rooftops,
faces of waiting women, endlessly,

walking the widows' walks waiting,
pacing the docks,
and searching out to the rocking sea

cradle of life
ocean endlessly rocking

For the Venus of Willendorf

ancient artifact 22,000 BCE

For a long time,
I've thought about this body of mine with agony,
with curiosity, and dreams of caressing lovers and children.
I've thought about these arms as if they
belonged to an Etruscan priestess, raising
them over her head to pray or protect hunters,
or were handles on the hips of an ancient
Greek vase displayed in the still light of a museum.
I've listened to the blood flowing through them
or crossed them over my breasts to imagine rest.
I've thought about these buttocks,
how they've held me to the earth
while others fly and inhabit high shelves of libraries.
I've thought about these peering nipples,
feelers on a cat's face sensitive to night.
Men accept mead, soma, nectar from my hands,
blood from my womb, fish from my eyes,
crystals from my eardrums,
food from my glands. In return,
they try to pierce the heart
that ticks between my thighs
pinning me to the bed like a butterfly.
These arms fly out of themselves to talk to you.
This head becomes small and sightless.
These breasts and buttocks swell
until they're all that's left of me, until
I'm melted into earth and planted as a garden.

The Origins of Milk

Despite the frenzy I've offered as love,
faces explode my albums
               with sighs that shatter gravestones.
Torn up for confetti, I'm showered
on the celebration winding in the streets below.

Another man is elected to rule the flow of milk.
I look for my mother copulating among sheep
in a dream field. A haze floats in over my head,
a long cold shore of sand.
I ask a genie waiting to be born
in blue smoke from my navel if
she has heard my magic words and knows
I, too, wish to see beyond the lamp.

All the telephones are out of order
in the soup of the city. Strange voices,
shells from unknown seas sound in my ears.
Stray dogs wander in gutters, nipping
at my toes. Abandoned children sit on curbs.
Panhandlers replace clowns on every corner.
They do not smile or dance, but simply ask
for money to be dropped in empty cups.
I ponder coins, weather maps,
rubber stamps, newsprint,
white bread, false hair, plutonium.

Stranded in a society of abstracted men,
I am made of primal customs

practiced in varied tongues.
I gather water, try to chat with you amidst
flower-boxes. Fumes clog my throat; machines
follow me down the street,
grinding gears against flesh. Links become unlinked
when I try to call you whom I met
by the accuracy of chance.
My eyes become glass blinded by headlights.

Blood I left on your sheets
came from moons of change hidden in my belly.
When we part, are you still there,

are we lovers as we were?
Curdling time gives us up to decisions.
Kettles whistle for morning coffee
and we mourn our dreams. I want
to bottle wind, drink it for cola. Instead,
I lose you among strange hands, open mouths,
wiggling buttocks, umbrellas.

I would have been what you were searching for
with sheer will, if you could decide
what sleeper you resemble and which of your dreams
struggles behind your eyelids.

I hardly bear the hollow music of a tubular life.
Birds in my inner ear batter wings to get out.
I have no names to call them to open windows.

The artful lover lacks artless feeling.
I knew when you touched me
where your thoughts were.
I can't be fooled into orgasm, but I can pretend.

Into my chest, I follow birds, trying to sing
proper notes to the moon, mirroring the sun,
to the darkness in me, nothing without your light.

Perhaps the finest language is silence in all its glory
as an apple tree standing in your garden?

To Lost and Found Love

> *. . . .in each of our mouths. There's that liquid river of story that sometimes sweeps us away . . . into the ha ha and the tender . . .*
> John Ribiki from *Three Lanterns*

In each of us is a story that starts deep
in the pain of the heart,
though some are lucky to have a story
that rises from sunny joy.

Usually, that joy comes from love,
but not always from a lover, perhaps,
even rarely from a lover,
more often from a parent who nurtured us,
and smiled lovingly at us.

Too often the story comes from purple sludge
at the bottom of the heart left there
by a lover or friend who disappointed us.
It's difficult for adults to get along
and play as children do.
Is a lack of innocence the problem?

Love that comes from the blue sunny pool of joy
at the top of the pumping heart
is the love of a child, or a grandparent
or a mother or father who gave
unselfishly to raise us up to a life
full of smiles that grow
like trees from the top of the red heart

over purple sludge at the bottom
that came from disappointed love

of a frightened, doomed lover
who gave up realizing

*Love is all there is,
is all we know of love!*

The Art of Loneliness

*Who are we when we are together
with no one but ourselves?*
                Hannah Arendt

We're born alone inside our skin;
we die alone inside our body,
and live inside our head.
Who hears our weeping
when our parents are gone
and we are old and widowed?
We don't cry to our children.
They have their own tears.

We embrace solitude and live
in a voiceless prison of self-talk.
Yet, aging in solitude we speak
more clearly to ourselves.
Loneliness makes an inner scream
deafening in its silence, loud enough
to sever the body from being.
The heart feels a heaviness
in the pulsing chest. The beating
evident in silence. How to break out
and trust in love somewhere?
We wade in rivers of memory
reliving the lives we remember we lived.
Daydreams are of past revelry or sorrow,
not thoughts of tomorrow.
What should I have done?
Should I have tried this or that
to keep love safely with me,
or was it just death of the ones I love,

that sequestered me, or the infidelity
of those I trusted that left me here
in stark intimacy with myself.
Is this room inside my head
more wisely furnished than it used to be?
Romance collapses early in life,
leaving one learning to trust bread,
when age shatters heat and leaves one
bone-deep in loneliness.
Living alone, wandering in memories,
one asks, "Do I like myself?
How can I live without intimacy?
Is there someone I should have been
who is better than who I've become?
How can I connect when I need to be alone
for my work?" Sex is not a cure for old people
too tired to be beautiful for it.

Technology traps me behind a screen.
Bedeviled by anguish,
I look to the gurus of loneliness.
None were happy with their solitude
if it continued day after day.

When solitude bears the fruit of art
 is it loneliness? Art can cure the grief
of loneliness turning it into solitude.
Do artists rebel from society,
feeling antagonistic, weary of the tasks of love,
all the imperfections, compromises of relationships,
that take time away from making art.

Is making art the art of loneliness?

Some Slippery Afternoon

A silver watch you've worn for years
is suddenly gone, leaving a pale
white stripe blazing on your wrist.

A calendar, marked with appointments
you meant to keep, disappears, leaving
a faded spot on the wall where it hung.

You search the house, yard, trash cans
for weeks, but never find it.

One night the glass in your windows
vanishes,
leaving you sitting in a gust of wind.

You think how a leg is suddenly lost
beneath a subway train, or taxi's wheel,
some slippery afternoon.

The child you've raised for years,
combing each lock, tailoring each smile,
each tear, each valuable thought,

suddenly changes to a harlequin,
joins the circus passing in the street,
never to be seen again.

One morning you wash your face,
look into the mirror, find the water
has eroded your features, worn them

smooth as a rock in a brook.
A blank-oval peers back at you
too mouthless to cry out.

Evening Hours Before Sleep

Ghostly words float in my brain
Gliding around in air and I fear hearing
them before sleep. They want
to speak of something left undone.

Did the rose blush too red,
and fill me with lost passion?
Did a forbidden memory cut
my finger as I carved the apple?
Is a lost friend eager to reach me?

Words hover around my head,
trying to descend onto my tongue
or rise from my lungs.
I'm interested in knowing
what those hovering words are
and where they've been.

Each day we die a little
with the setting of the sun.
Each day, a day older until
years sink below the horizon
leaving us old in each other's eyes.
Yet still, I hope to love more,
letting feelings blossom
like sunflowers named for rising suns.

I can still recall my young face
smiling with a corporal twinkle.
Nothing quite completely disappears
under the blanket of memory

for as long as we can remember,
like the salt marsh at high tide,
that comes and goes, and brings things in
leaving them behind in wet sand.

Too many people scribbling on each other's tongues
gag the cities. Politics muddle the nature of bodies.
Sexual energy, a force confused, wasted.
Longing for the clear heat of truth
in these witching hours,
I have a pleasant dream of a land inhabited by bright animals
who refuse fire and eat nothing but leaves.

Rejection Makes Wings
with Each Little Death It Offers

I've known rejection as much anyone.
The love I yearned for escaped on that winged horse
who always flies higher as we reach higher and higher,
heaven always beyond grasp.

I've reached for love with words, longed for love,
hoping to live forever in books, enjoying the attempt
in those moments when we know we're alive,
and words fall into music that engulfs the smiles
of those who want nuance, more than sound that blasts
the mind with dance.

Still, what I've swallowed of love sticks in my throat
with a bitter glue of longing, as love happens
only in moments that pass like ripples
over cloudy skies that hide the sun,
giving shade enough to make desire blaze.

Envious gods want to pick at our flesh,
so we're not allowed to live forever,
but hope our love like Dickinson's or Millay's
could live in poems that sharpen mortality.

Sometimes I feel my words are mere trash
sitting in the rain, waiting to be collected
before it spills into the gutter and runs down
drains at the ends of streets into nowhere.
We're often trying to love, and not loving,
but we're trying, and when we stop trying, we're dead,

even as poems that live sting us with memories of lovers
who are gone with their words longing for a love,
so good, so pure, so erotic with touch once felt,
that it flees onto a page, or off into graves, or up flying
after that winged horse
who always goes higher, up and away
into the land of Pegasus green pastures
    where we can never go
        until we fly chasing
            after that heavenly tail.

Peopled with the Dead

Peopled now in these waning years with dead
friends and lovers who once cared for me,
but now can't still my restless spirit,
or share regrets in terrifying spring,
or sorrowful winter,
that comes again, turning seasons
                              in wonders.

I walk with their faces, their tears and laughter,
images etched before my eyes,
their smiles or sighs, felt
memories of their hands in mine, their voices
echo in ravenous time creeping
over my face in lines marked by their dying,
their thoughts and dreams defining mine.

There is no longing so complete
as the desire to talk with the dead.

Is there survivor's guilt after the pandemic

when so many, young and old are gone
before their time, wilted away
because a narcissistic sadist
was our president.

If we weren't living, we couldn't feel anything,
so, what good is survivor's guilt
and what about empathy for the dead,
when we don't know if they can feel it?

Is guilt always a condition of the living,
when so many are dead and dying
all the time, but especially
during a pandemic, and horribly in wars?

It's the living left behind,
it's we left bereft
with our love in our warm hands,
a hollow hallowed offering
to the dead
who live only in memory?

In living memories
our dead live on and on
as we wonder,
who will keep us alive
in their minds?
The trouble is too many evil ones
live on in our minds, in infamous

memory—cluttering up the space.
Atilla the Hun, Hitler, Stalin, Putin . . .

Is it clear as sunlight filled crystal,
or obvious to say the way to live,
hopefully and happily
is to remember
the ones who lived lovingly?

We know who they are,
for each of us,
and we say their names
longingly.

Spring has come again!

It's an old tune, they say,
but I say,
the heart must learn it anew.
Chickadees, mourning doves and cardinals
pecked amidst winter berries and pines,
but soon the ruby-throated humming bird
will come again to flight among honeysuckle blooms.
A new calf will be born in the woods on the hill
and a pregnant doe will nibble our crocuses
before they're full.
Spring has come again.
It's an old tune, they say,
but I say,
The heart must learn it anew.

As When Some Silenced Singer Hears Her Aria

A Sonnet for Vittoria Colonna,* Naples, Ischia, 1492-1547

or creatures crawl riding foam to hurry back to salty home,
as oceans pound fruit to pecking pipers,
or shells keep tunes in ear-like chambers,
filled with sand and sea to roam
like songs rejoicing feathered nest and comb
as warm eggs crack chirping hunger, and children slither
forth to touch, smell, see, hear earthly cries and laughter
pushed suckling free from nurturing womb –

my tongue is loosed beyond a private caroling, my pen prances
urged by mysterious love as if it had no part in what is sighed
as Earth sings praises through me,
my eyes: green sea, red skies, wildflowers,
a child who dances when loved
beyond the pain of men's tribal wars, pride,
threatened suicide, and bloody rivalry.

---

* Vittoria Colonna was (1490 -1547) was an Italian poet and inspiration to Michelangelo. As an educated, married noblewoman whose husband was in captivity, she wrote poetry that attracted attention in the late 1510's and ultimately became one of the most popular poets of 16th-century Italy. Upon the early death of her husband, she took refuge at a convent in Rome. She was the first woman of Europe to publish a widely read book of poetry.

Imagine all the pounding hearts

pumping billions of gallons of blood,
lakes of tears, echoes of laughter!
Imagine more than eight billion
human lives throbbing.
And the rhythms inside rocks,
rhythms of atoms spinning,
planets circling in space,
clocks ticking, rhythms of tides
obeying the moon. Worlds turning
in trillions of universes expanding,
spinning with their burning stars exploding,
and here on our small planet *Earth*,
our rock home full of molten gasses,
people arguing, killing each other over their gods.

A grandmother combs the hair of a child.
Her hands move in rhythms of water
running over stones and pebbles,
flowing like love to thirsty mouths.

The creosote on fence posts beneath the earth
keeps them standing, but wood finally rots
as worms chew in the rhythm of clouds
floating across skies changing shapes
viewed like Rorschach tests by those
who look up dreaming into endless blue.
There are secrets hidden in throats of caves,
crying screams in waterfalls, rustling leaves,
stirrings under them, the dead reborn as grass.
All wondered by each life among the billions as one
merges into another, as one hand picks up a book

between thumb and fingers and reads the time of galaxies, crustaceans, primates since Earth began four point five billion years ago and humans arriving merely 200 thousand years ago, now destroying our habitat, Earth and all her feeling, mammalian hearts pumping billions of gallons of blood.

III.
STARDUST LIVES IN US

*I'm not afraid of dying.
I was dead for thousands of years before I was born,
and it never caused me the slightest inconvenience.*

Mark Twain

*Stardust thou art, and into stardust
thou shalt return.*

Lionel B. Luttinger

The Blue Whale

There's so much truth of Earth unknown to us,
composed 60% of oceans.
We know so little science of creatures,
newly discovered each year
who live in Earth's deepest watery depths.

Dolphins leap and play forming swells
far out in mid-ocean that help power
huge waves that travel rolling toward the shore,
starting in small swells approaching beaches
curling over, rising, crashing and breaking.

Swimming deep with a heart big as a railway car,
the blue whale, fastest animal of the sea, sounds up.
It can attain a streamlined length of 106 feet
and 150 tons. Toothless, it sucks 2 tons of food
straining it through a series of baleen plates,
yet its throat is only a few inches wide! It can't swallow
anything bigger than sardines, krill or plankton.
We've lived by myths. Jonah could not enter into its belly.

The giant blue mammal, largest being on earth
lives only 20 years, taking 11 months to form a calf of 3 tons—
nursing for 8 months and growing at a rate of 2 tons a day.
Without arctic waters where it breeds the giant mammal
cannot live. Only ten or twenty thousand may be left.

The giant blue whale lives on threatened plankton,
riddled with disintegrating plastic bits,

a mammal like us breathing our atmospheric air.

We've threatened its being
even before we've understood its songs,
its poetry, its mysterious life.

When History's Truth Is Amazing Grace

On one small planet of green trees and blue waters that give life—
among aloof stars, supernovas exploding fire near and far—
we're one species of many cultures and colors
traveling in endless space, amid indifferent stars,
on our tiny Earth as she floats toward Vega,
a far-off ending, result unknown.

Lies collide with eco-logic as battlefields bloom with blood.
Soldiers rot in foreign soil where medieval religions collide.
If the screaming bombs and bullets of arrogant dictators
could be silenced, we'd hear the children's cries
of hunger, we'd hear truth singing in our brains.
We'd stop waving warring flags,
to raise a universal flag of blue-green Earth,
waving above peace where all wars have ceased.

When the competitive mumblings in temples,
mosques and churches ends in ecumenical praise,
we'll tremble with happiness among singing birds,
the masses degrading gold, as water becomes more precious.
We'd laugh as children reveling in forests, flowers, fruits.
In psychic peace, anger released breathing deeply,
free of hate, we'd smile at babies of many colors.

Weapons destroyed, land mines removed,
aroma of burning flesh and forests
gone from the nostrils of truth,
and dreams free of nightmares,
children could dress their dolls in flags of truce
while elders walk in peaceful evenings,
and all dream tranquilly free of nightmares.

We'll know that not the Gardens of Babylon,
or Stonehenge, or the gods of Easter Island,
or the Pyramids, not The Eiffel Tower, The Great Wall,
or the Empire State Building are the truest wonders,
of our human history, but the ability to love, to feel empathy,
makes us the *paragon of animals*:
one humanity on one small swirling planet,
gifted by Mother Earth and Father Sky,
Sister Sea and Brother Forest— not punished by eating
bright apples of the *Tree of Knowledge*, but all of us
born of the same green, breathing *Tree of Life*

Yes, to Life

Trees are the oldest living beings on Earth,
There are 80,000-year-old groves of Quick Aspens
And 13,000-year-old Eucalyptus Trees. 3,000-year-old
ancient redwoods, and giant sequoias of California are
threatened by climate fires. Time was long
for trees who give us breath and food,
and short for us living things whose use
of fossilized fuel is killing them. We're polluting life
with long ago death of trees and animals. What irony!

We will only have from living what we expect from it.
Poets can tell the world how to treat life,
because if the greedy world tells us, we're in trouble
as we are now, committing *Ecocide,*
burning Earth's dead matter, oil of rotted dinosaurs
and tar from ancient vegetation underground,
dirty energy burned, killing the trees and us.

So, the good of poetry now is to love trees
who feed us with breath, shelter,
 and shade us, as we speak for ourselves
to live in peace with trees.

There is faith in living fiercely
 to love the children who are our life
hereafter. I am thinking of what we feel
we are worthy of in this world.

Since the dawn of time, trees
have been our silent companions.
They bear steadfast witness to our earthly lives

while reaching up toward the heavens. We
ask them for answers and they answer
with comforting green beauty, food and shade,
and exchange breath with us in *atmospheric balance*.
Without their companionship there is no life,
and they are burning up.
I am an old woman who walks every morning
under the trees who talk to me of love,
and how we are all preparing to leave
love and life to the children and I ask
what are we doing to save them?

The trees are dying

for Georgia Spaw, Forester

"It's true." the forester sighed.
"Sugar maples are disappearing.
Too many toxic chemicals!
Trees sunlit. Trees moonlit. Trees wet
with rain, covered in snow.
First green in spring, are dying like us
in climate crisis.

The last view for everyone, should be of trees.
Trees are all to us, the origins of food, of milk,
first link in the food chain
that binds mammals to Earth.

Bartlett pear trees, with their sweet golden fruit
dropping from glossy green branches,
leaves with fringes folded inward like arms
on a dying breast. Apple trees in orchards
on the horizon. Hazelnut, hickory, poplar, rock oak,
blue spruce, juniper, red cedar, yewberry, ashberry,
red oak and white oak, red pine and grey pine,
rare elms and douglas furs, redwoods cut for timber,
phenomenal ancient *Giant Sequoia* felled
for picnic tables and chairs. Rainforests murdered
for grazing meat!" The forester looked out the window
from her bed. "A 30 percent decline and a loss
of nearly half of new trees over the past
forty years. Synthetic chemicals begin to appear
in their rings at the dawn of the Industrial Revolution—
poisons traced to the Ohio River Valley, airborne
to the Northeastern forests…."

She murmurs as she slips into her forever sleep:
"Seeds of the endangered white bark pine of the Rockies,
staple of bears, red squirrels, song birds are disappearing.
The dark green aromatic hemlocks are falling to a blight,
wooly adelgid scale, which also invites
infestation by spider mites. So, the Eastern Hemlocks go
the way of the American Elm from its disease,
and the American Chestnut before them perished too.
The trees are going to entropy, acid rain, chemicals
P.C.B.s, pesticides." She sighs, murmuring:

"The trees are all that comfort me.
They hold all the answers unspoken in their branches.

Trees make time visible and fragrant. They breathe
with us. They are our breath as we breathe out
we are their life. As they live we breathe with them
in atmospheric balance and live by their photosynthesis
and our greed for things is killing them. Trees
hold all the answers unspoken in their branches.

We enter the grove and are changed, peace rains
down in green over us. Green that holds mountains
together with roots, green that scatters lacey shade
over us, spins out our breath in freshened sips.

We drink the rain with them. Beware, the trees
are dying with us. Every sapling rises up to breathe
with every child in its rightful place under the sun.
Please, set me free into the arms of a weeping beech tree!"

Oh Gaia, Dear Mother

I've been out in the streets marching, organizing, preaching
to save you for the children. I've been out in the streets,
a grandmother marching, and now I sit in comfort tired
and thinking of refugees fleeing bloody battlefields
brought on by a revolutions and invasions,
exacerbated by drought in farmlands intensified
by climate crisis and global warming.

Five million climate refugees are expected yearly now,
and I could live in comfort except for the pain I feel
looking into the eyes of children, beckoning to me,
filling my eyes with burning tears.
I cannot enjoy my "Golden Years"
unless they speak of shade, rice, wheat, apples,
fruits you've given us at time of harvest,
of Thanksgiving. How we're destroying your bounty
meant for children. I grieve our consuming greed,
but what good is my anger? What good is my preaching?
What good is my compassion for our enemies?

You've given us, Mother, all the milk and honey,
and music we live by could be done and finished
unless we learn to love and respect you as our sustenance
here in your raging winds, churning waters, warming sun.

Turning into Light

Light split me open
when I left my cage of dreams.

I was sent to view the stars.
made of the dust of us. I turned
into something sweeter.

Love burst wide open
into a booming galaxy, untied.

I became free in awe
of a wonderful secret.
Pure love can flow
from an infinite light out there.

My beloved never fulfilled my life,
but that was only a fraction
of a promise written in my heart.

A divine seed was planted in my psyche
in a fertile meadow
belonging to the universe.

I looked again within myself,
and discovered the awe
of creation and my spirit

bloomed in knowing
that I am not meant to know
the secrets of eternity.

I am only meant to feel
an infinite ecstasy, and understand
that a real religion

is the flowering of lovers, who
nurture truly,
creating new life
One from two.
A child born from love
heals the mysterious universe!

A Dreaming Child Comes to Me in My Dream

She's dreaming I'm Queen of Her Dream in mine,
and she enters my throne room dressed in rainbows.
She offers me a perfect stone in her small hand.

"Please don't leave me an Earth of rocks,
no matter how round or perfect," she pleads.
"I'll need green food and blue water
from white mountain streams for my sisters
and brothers to swim in time."

Around her small head, a colored halo glows.-
With her dress of rainbow sun-light she's made
all of light so bright my aged eyes tear, purple
rivers streaming down my face, falling in my hands
upturned like dead birds in my lap, a cup for her stone.

"I'll need green breath with sunlit food
for my life to glow on forever with sisters and brothers,
child after child from child after child," she begs.

The stone, now wet, she's put in my hand wriggles alive,
a silvery fish with a golden eye. It leaps from my lap
into her hands. She drifts away with her shining fish,
in her river of light to a land of bright fruits that I, the Queen
of Her Dream in my dream, bestow upon her flowing
in her rainbow alight with a river of forever children,
laughing, drinking, swimming, singing.

Liberty and Justice

As a schoolgirl, I put my hand over my heart
to pledge allegiance to the flag
of The United States of America,
before I learned about the stealing of native lands,
history of slavery, hatred toward immigrants,
even my compassionate, hardworking father
a maligned Italian immigrant, called
wop, guinea, dago, spaghetti-bender.

We pledged allegiance at the start of every school day
in the ghetto classrooms of Newark and Irvington
New Jersey where the "colored kids' were put
in back rows where teachers always parked them
and ignored them, as if Black lives didn't matter.

The flag hung from a pole over the dusty blackboard
in the corner of the grubby room
where we learned our ABC's. One day, lost
on the way to school, I wandered from the Italian
and Jewish ghetto into the Black one.

There I saw tired old men sitting dejectedly
on dilapidated porches, broken windows with torn shades.
I looked like Shirley Temple in my blue homemade dress,
my blond curls bouncing as I hurried, scared
to find my way. My Mary Jane patent leather shoes
clicked along the cracked pavements, but no one
bothered me. They just looked at me as if to say,
  "Why are you walking here, little white girl?"
Our *Pledge of Allegiance* always ended

with "one nation under God, *indivisible*,
with liberty and justice
for all."

We're Stardust and Water

and all the stardust,
and water of which we're made
has always been here since
The Big Bang.

Some water of which you're made
might have been in Walt Whitman
or Emily Dickinson, Einstein, Vivaldi,
Bach, Lady Murasaki, Martin Luther King, Jr.,
or Eleanor Roosevelt ….

But where did the first hydrogen molecule
come from,
and what happened before
The Big Bang?
No one knows.

We're made of stardust
with water that's always recycling.
Do we need more mystery
than that?

Sounds of traffic poisoning the air
wake me from fitful sleep like a dirge.
Is the world ending, my species dying off
from over-population, pollution, greed,
burning of trees?

Old trees sequester tons of carbon,
our speech as we exhale
is our words of love and hate

breathed out as carbon dioxide
that trees take in giving us oxygen.

My soul lives in the burning forest.
My heart beats too slowly from pain,
too often broken by disappointed love,
betrayal, jealousy, envy, hurt.

Are we worthy of creation?
I look at others I meet:
One who is young and full of sorrow
lives in agony for her dead husband.
Another's gay son is dead from AIDS,
and has a sister who hates her,
my nurse in New York City was hit by a drunk
driver and hurled in the air landing on the street.
There's the one fighting cancer whose lover left him
as he struggles through chemo.
The pretty woman's father is dying of Alzheimer's,
while her mother has breast cancer.
My newest friend's husband just had a stroke.
The blind art historian can no longer see art.

Everywhere we look there's pain.
I can't find one without some.
My many books praised by critics
sit in the drawer or on library shelves.
Who are they saving?

The world seems slowly ending
in agony. Psychologists talk
of a new mental disease, *ecological grief,*
environmental depression
among the young who want no children
brought forth to die in tsunami, tornados,
superstorms, floods, droughts, starvation, thirst.

Five million refugees yearly climatologists warn us,
while some lying leaders are traitors to country and Earth,
we try to live a doctrine of love praying prayers
that seem unheard, but *Keep Hope Alive*,
as outer space is full of exploding stars, spraying
the stardust of which we're made,

We're stardust
alive by the magic of clean water,
running out everywhere,
yet, with an inch of time to save ourselves.

Big-hearted, Witty and Wide-Eyed

Earth! She's been around for about 4.5 billion years,
and the first third of Her billions were mayhem:
Meteorites crashed into Her. Magma everywhere,
acid rain falling on Her, until finally,
Her first wildlife, fungi, started forming,
then only single-celled ocean critters
for another third of those billions of years.

Sex life didn't show up for nearly another third
of the billions of years in a *Precambrian Age,*
plant-animals with weird fronds
and sea-tubes copulating like sea-horses.

Trilobites paddled around for a few billion years
more, until ancient forests grew and dinosaurs
crunched through Her trees,
chewing Her photosynthesizing leaves.

We mammals have been here a very short time.
Before us came primates, orangutans, chimps,
Neanderthals, arrowheads, Cleopatra
and then the naming of stars by Greeks.

And you and I, with our DVDs, Smart Phones,
shelved books, our masquerade costumes, shoes,
regrets, dreams, hopes, mouths we've kissed,
or wished we'd kissed—have only been here for a
microscopic bit of time, a slice of time so comparatively
thin you'd need a microscope to see it.
Just take a file off that bit of time and you'd wipe out

Shakespeare, ancient Greece and the Bible,
to say nothing of all those hundreds of Hollywood flicks.

We're each no more than an illuminated mote,
dancing in a beam of light for a second that's passing away,
insignificant amid crowds of over 8 billion living today,
and billions dying yesterday? So, I say:

"Be big-hearted, witty and wide-eyed with wonder!
Read about the *Anthropocene Age*, love some others,
paint, sing, taste everything lawfully possible,
and help save the kids from Climate Crisis,
because you still have some hours left!"

Acknowledgments

"As When Some Silenced Singer Hears Her Aria." *Sparrow: A Journal of the Sonnet,* ed. Felix Stefanile. West Lafayette Indiana: Purdue University, 1996. *Chelsea Lit. Rev.* 78 (2005): 55-7,

"As When Some Silenced Singer Hears Her Aria." *Confrontation at Twenty* 37/38 (1988): 223.

_____. *Sparrow* 63 (Oct. 1996): 103.

"As When Some Silenced Singer Hears Her Aria," "The House," and "The Young Child." *Chelsea Lit. Rev.* 78 (2005): 55-7.

"Beyond the East Gate." *The Nation* 219.10 (1974): 316.

"Big Blue Ball Wet with Sun." *Nature. mini-Mag: outside the ordinary;* New York (2006).

"Big Hearted, Witty, and Wide-Eyed" *Waging Beauty as the Polar Bear Dreams of Ice*, PWP, Hoboken, NJ, 2016. Also: audio for a video-poems by videographer Ellery J Sampson at https://www.youtube.com/@danielagioseffi579

"Billions of Gallons of Blood." *Forever Night: Siempre Noche - The Alternative New Year's Day Spoken Word / Performance Extravaganza!* (2017): 21.

"Carbon Summer or Nuclear Winter." *Robert Frost Foundation*, Facebook page, with audio recitation by author, archived at *Sound Cloud*, And Honorable Mention Award, May 8th, 2015. Also in *Waging Beauty*, PWP, Hoboken, NY 2016.

"Carbon Summer or Nuclear War." *Academia.edu.* 2016.

"Catastrophic Carousel of Greed," Audio for a video-poem by Ellery J. Sampson, https://www.youtube.com/@danielagioseffi579

_____. *The Poetry Corner.* Ed. by Chris Butters. 1 Jul. 2014.

"Chant for the Water Protectors at Standing Rock." *Poeming Pigeon* 4.1 No. 7 (2018): 91-2

"Earth's Body in True Genesis." *Star in the Fire: Anthology of the Alternative New Year's Day Spoken Word Extravaganza.* New York: A.N.Y.D.S.W.P.E. Imprint

Excerpts from "The Last Fire Feast." *Atomic Ghost: Poets Respond to the Nuclear Age.* Ed. John Bradley. Minneapolis: Coffee House P, 1995. 140.

"Maggots and Wheat." *Sundial: A Lit. Rev. of Columbia U* 3.1 (1969): 43.

"Mother Earth, *Gaia.*" *Brownstone Poets:* Patricia Carrigan, ed. New York, NY, (2017). Audio for a video created by Anton Evangelista for the docudrama *Author and Activist*: The Daniela Gioseffi Story. https://www.youtube.com/@danielagioseffi579

_____. Also: https//www.EcoPoetry.org Audio for a video-poem by videographer Omar M'Sai at https://www.youtube.com/@danielagioseffi579

"Mother Earth, You Are a City of Lilies and Applet Trees," Audio for a video-poem with videography by Ellery J. Sampson. https://www.youtube.com/@danielagioseffi579

"One Wet Planet." *Manorborn Issue #* 71. (2009): p.57.

"Our Small Blue Dot" published as a video-poem with videography by Gaynor Lowell on https://www.youtube.com/@danielagioseffi579

"Some Slippery Afternoon." *Amer. Voices.* Ed. Hans P. Guth. Lexington, MA: D.C. Heath and Co., 1981. 332.

_____. *Cries of the Spirit: A Celebration of Women's Spirituality.* Ed. Marilyn Sewell. Boston: Beacon P, 1991. 120-1.

_____. *Literature: Options for Reading and Writing.* Eds. Donald A. Daiker, Mary Fuller, and Jack E. Wallace. 1st ed. New York: Harper, 1985. 609.

_____. 2nd Edition. New York: Harper, 1989. 816.

"Some Slippery Afternoon," "Through the Eye of the Needle," and "Eggs." *Ardis Anthology of New Amer. Poets.* Eds. Ellendea Proffer and David Rigsbee, eds. Ann Arbor: Ardis, 1977. 116-9.

"Some Slippery Afternoon." *White Ink: Poems on Mothers and Motherhood.* Ed. Rishma Dunlop. Toronto: Demeter P, 2007. 89.

"The Origins of Milk." *The Milk of Almonds: Amer. Women Writers on Food and Culture.* Louise DeSalvo and Edvige Giunta, eds. New York: Feminist Press, City U of NY (2002) 121-3. Also in *Choice: A Mag. of Poetry and Graphics.* SUNY, Buffalo, NY, 7/8 (1972): 67-73.

"The Trees Are Dying: Origins of Milk" *Klimaaksjon: Norwegian Writers Climate Plan* https://forfatternesklimaaksjon.no/the-origins-of-milk/ (Jan. 2014)

"The Plan." *New Verse News* (26 Nov. 2013). *Riding the Meridian, New York, NY.* Also, a Video Poem with Videography by Omar M'Sai. https://www.youtube.com/@danielagioseffi579

"The Weighty Everlasting Wait of Waiting Women." *Phoebus, Vol. 3 No. 2, Hampton, VA. 1986.*

"Liberty and Justice," Winner of the South Orange/Maplewood FLAG DAY event. Chosen to be read at *Spiotta Memorial Park Rally,* June 14th, 2025..

About the Author

DANIELA GIOSEFFI is an American Book Award winning author of 18 books of poetry and prose. She edits *EcoPoetry.org*, which receives 6 thousand global visitors monthly. She's published in *The Nation, The Paris Review, Prairie Schooner, Poetry International, Rain Taxi Review, Chelsea Literary Review* and in many magazines and anthologies, e.g. Oxford U. Press: *Stories of the American Experience.* Her first of six books of poetry was *Eggs in the Lake* (BOA Editions, 1979). Poems therein won a NY State Council for the Arts Grant Award. Her latest books of poetry are *Waging Beauty* (PWP, 2016) and *Blood Autumn: Autunno di Sangue* (Bordighera Press, 2007) the year in which she won The John Ciardi Award for Lifetime Achievement in Poetry. In 2008, Daniela won the Order the Sons of Italy NY State Literary Award. In 2003, she was given an American Italian Educators Lifetime Achievement Award.

Her women's studies classic *Women on War: International Writings* (Touchstone/ Simon & Schuster, 1988, and The Feminist Press, NY, 2003) has been in print for over 37 years. She published *On Prejudice: A Global Perspective* (Anchor Doubleday, 1993) to win a World Peace Prize from The Ploughshares Fund, presented at the U.N. Her work appears in anthologies from Harper Collins, Viking, Penguin Books, etc. Her verse was etched in marble near that of Walt Whitman's and William Carlos Williams's on a wall of PENN Station, NY City, 2002. She's presented on WNYC, NPR the BBC, and appeared on CBS & NBC.

Daniela won PEN American Center's Syndicated Fiction Award for *Daffodil Dollars*, aired on The Sound of Words, hosted by Alan Cheuse. She published three novels, her latest an e-book titled *The Story of Emily Dickinson's "Master."* In 2013, *VIA* Folios/Bordighera Press published *Pioneering Italian American Culture: Essays & Interviews* with an introduction and notes by Angelina Oberdan.

Her work's been translated into Italian, Spanish, German, Serbo-Croation, Chinese and Japanese. A docu-drama of her life *Author and Activist*, by award winning filmmaker Anton Evangelista, premiered at the Maya Daren Theater in Manhattan in 2014 and has been screening on campuses from Hofstra to St. Johns U. to St. Francis College, and The Calandra Institute of CUNY. She was featured at international book fairs from Barcelona to Miami. More information is available at: The Poetry Foundation of America, The Academy of American Poets, and on The Poet and the Poem, Radio Show Hosted by Grace Cavalieri at The Library of Congress, and The National Endowment for the Arts. More information can be found at https://www.DanielaGioseffi.com and www.AuthorandActivist.com. Daniela's video poems can be viewed at https://www.youtube.com/@danielagioseffi579

VIA FOLIOS
A refereed book series dedicated to the culture of Italians and Italian Americans.

CARLA PANCIERA. *One Trail of Longing, Another of String*. Vol. 185. Poetry.
LIBBY CATALDI. *It Takes a Lifetime to Learn How to Live*. Vol. 184. Memoir.
DANIELLE JONES. Hunger. Vol. 183. Poetry.
GIOSE RIMANELLI. *Benedetta in Guysterland*. Vol. 182. Literature.
DANTE DI STEFANO. *The Widowing Radiance*. Vol. 181. Poetry.
ANNA MONARDO. *The Courtyard of Dreams*. Vol. 180. Novel.
MATTHEW CARIELLO. *Colloquy of Mad Tom*. Vol. 179. Poetry.
GRACE CAVALIERI. *Fables from Italy and Beyond*. Vol. 178. Poetry.
LAURETTE FOLK. *Eleison*. Vol. 177. Novel.
FRANCES NEVILL. *Coquina Soup*. Vol. 176. Literature.
FRANCINE MASIELLO. *The Tomb of the Divers*. Vol. 175. Novel.
PIETRO DI DONATO. *Collected Stories*. Vol. 174. Literature.
RACHEL GUIDO DeVRIES. *The Birthday Years*. Vol. 173. Poetry.
MATTHEW MEDURI. *Collegiate Gothic*. Vol. 172. Novel.
THOMAS RUGGIO. *Finding Dandini*. Vol. 171. Art History.
TAMBURRI GIORDANO GARDAPHÈ. *From the Margin*. Vol. 170. Anthology.
ANNA MONARDO. *After Italy*. Vol. 169. Memoir.
JOEY NICOLETTI. *Extinction Wednesday*. Vol. 168. Poetry.
MARIA FAMÀ. *Trigger*. Vol. 167. Poetry.
WILLI Q MINN. *What? Nothing*. Vol. 166. Poetry.
RICHARD VETERE. *She's Not There*. Vol. 165. Literature.
FRANK GIOIA. *Mercury Man*. Vol. 164. Literature.
LUISA M. GIULIANETTI. *Agrodolce*. Vol. 163. Literature.
ANGELO ZEOLLA. *The Bronx Unbound ovvero i versi bronxesi*. Vol. 162. Poetry.
NICHOLAS A. DiCHARIO. *Giovanni's Tree*. Vol. 161. Literature.
ADELE ANNESI. *What She Takes Away*. Vol. 160. Novel.
ANNIE RACHELE LANZILLOTTO. *Whaddyacall the Wind?*. Vol. 159. Memoir.
JULIA LISELLA. *Our Lively Kingdom*. Vol. 158. Poetry.
MARK CIABATTARI. *When the Mask Slips*. Vol. 157. Novel.
JENNIFER MARTELLI. *The Queen of Queens*. Vol. 156. Poetry.
TONY TADDEI. *The Sons of the Santorelli*. Vol. 155. Literature.
FRANCO RICCI. *Preston Street • Corso Italias*. Vol. 154. History.
MIKE FIORITO. *The Hated Ones*. Vol. 153. Literature.
PATRICIA DUNN. *Last Stop on the 6*. Vol. 152. Novel.
WILLIAM BOELHOWER. *Immigrant Autobiography*. Vol. 151. Literary Criticism.
MARC DIPAOLO. *Fake Italian*. Vol. 150. Literature.
GAIL REITANO. *Italian Love Cake*. Vol. 149. Novel.
VINCENT PANELLA. *Sicilian Dreams*. Vol. 148. Novel.
MARK CIABATTARI. *The Literal Truth: Rizzoli Dreams of Eating the Apple of Earthly Delights*. Vol. 147. Novel.
MARK CIABATTARI. *Dreams of An Imaginary New Yorker Named Rizzoli*. Vol. 146. Novel.

LAURETTE FOLK. *The End of Aphrodite*. Vol. 145. Novel.
ANNA CITRINO. *A Space Between*. Vol. 144. Poetry
MARIA FAMÀ. *The Good for the Good*. Vol. 143. Poetry.
ROSEMARY CAPPELLO. *Wonderful Disaster*. Vol. 142. Poetry.
B. AMORE. *Journeys on the Wheel*. Vol. 141. Poetry.
ALDO PALAZZESCHI. *The Manifestos of Aldo Palazzeschi*. Vol 140. Literature.
ROSS TALARICO. *The Reckoning*. Vol 139. Poetry.
MICHELLE REALE. *Season of Subtraction*. Vol 138. Poetry.
MARISA FRASCA. *Wild Fennel*. Vol 137. Poetry.
RITA ESPOSITO WATSON. *Italian Kisses*. Vol. 136. Memoir.
SARA FRUNER. *Bitter Bites from Sugar Hills*. Vol. 135. Poetry.
KATHY CURTO. *Not for Nothing*. Vol. 134. Memoir.
JENNIFER MARTELLI. *My Tarantella*. Vol. 133. Poetry.
MARIA TERRONE. *At Home in the New World*. Vol. 132. Essays.
GIL FAGIANI. *Missing Madonnas*. Vol. 131. Poetry.
LEWIS TURCO. *The Sonnetarium*. Vol. 130. Poetry.
JOE AMATO. *Samuel Taylor's Hollywood Adventure*. Vol. 129. Novel.
BEA TUSIANI. *Con Amore*. Vol. 128. Memoir.
MARIA GIURA. *What My Father Taught Me*. Vol. 127. Poetry.
STANISLAO PUGLIESE. *A Century of Sinatra*. Vol. 126. Popular Culture.
TONY ARDIZZONE. *The Arab's Ox*. Vol. 125. Novel.
PHYLLIS CAPELLO. *Packs Small Plays Big*. Vol. 124. Literature.
FRED GARDAPHÉ. *Read 'em and Reap*. Vol. 123. Criticism.
JOSEPH A. AMATO. *Diagnostics*. Vol 122. Literature.
DENNIS BARONE. *Second Thoughts*. Vol 121. Poetry.
OLIVIA K. CERRONE. *The Hunger Saint*. Vol 120. Novella.
GARIBLADI M. LAPOLLA. *Miss Rollins in Love*. Vol 119. Novel.
JOSEPH TUSIANI. *A Clarion Call*. Vol 118. Poetry.
JOSEPH A. AMATO. *My Three Sicilies*. Vol 117. Poetry & Prose.
MARGHERITA COSTA. *Voice of a Virtuosa and Coutesan*. Vol 116. Poetry.
NICOLE SANTALUCIA. *Because I Did Not Die*. Vol 115. Poetry.
MARK CIABATTARI. *Preludes to History*. Vol 114. Poetry.
HELEN BAROLINI. *Visits*. Vol 113. Novel.
ERNESTO LIVORNI. *The Fathers' America*. Vol 112. Poetry.
MARIO B. MIGNONE. *The Story of My People*. Vol 111. Non-fiction.
GEORGE GUIDA. *The Sleeping Gulf*. Vol 110. Poetry.
JOEY NICOLETTI. *Reverse Graffiti*. Vol 109. Poetry.
GIOSE RIMANELLI. *Il mestiere del furbo*. Vol 108. Criticism.
LEWIS TURCO. *The Hero Enkidu*. Vol 107. Poetry.
AL TACCONELLI. *Perhaps Fly*. Vol 106. Poetry.
RACHEL GUIDO DEVRIES. *A Woman Unknown in Her Bones*. Vol 105. Poetry.
BERNARD BRUNO. *A Tear and a Tear in My Heart*. Vol 104. Non-fiction.
FELIX STEFANILE. *Songs of the Sparrow*. Vol 103. Poetry.
FRANK POLIZZI. *A New Life with Bianca*. Vol 102. Poetry.
GIL FAGIANI. *Stone Walls*. Vol 101. Poetry.
LOUISE DESALVO. *Casting Off*. Vol 100. Fiction.

MARY JO BONA. *I Stop Waiting for You.* Vol 99. Poetry.
RACHEL GUIDO DEVRIES. *Stati zitt, Josie.* Vol 98. Children's Literature. $8
GRACE CAVALIERI. *The Mandate of Heaven.* Vol 97. Poetry.
MARISA FRASCA. *Via incanto.* Vol 96. Poetry.
DOUGLAS GLADSTONE. *Carving a Niche for Himself.* Vol 95. History.
MARIA TERRONE. *Eye to Eye.* Vol 94. Poetry.
CONSTANCE SANCETTA. *Here in Cerchio.* Vol 93. Local History.
MARIA MAZZIOTTI GILLAN. *Ancestors' Song.* Vol 92. Poetry.
MICHAEL PARENTI. *Waiting for Yesterday: Pages from a Street Kid's Life.* Vol 90. Memoir.
ANNIE LANZILLOTTO. *Schitsong.* Vol 89. Poetry.
EMANUEL DI PASQUALE. *Love Lines.* Vol 88. Poetry.
CAROSONE & LOGIUDICE. *Our Naked Lives.* Vol 87. Essays.
JAMES PERICONI. *Strangers in a Strange Land: A Survey of Italian-Language American Books.* Vol 86. Book History.
DANIELA GIOSEFFI. *Escaping La Vita Della Cucina.* Vol 85. Essays.
MARIA FAMÀ. *Mystics in the Family.* Vol 84. Poetry.
ROSSANA DEL ZIO. *From Bread and Tomatoes to Zuppa di Pesce "Ciambotto".* Vol. 83. Memoir.
LORENZO DELBOCA. *Polentoni.* Vol 82. Italian Studies.
SAMUEL GHELLI. *A Reference Grammar.* Vol 81. Italian Language.
ROSS TALARICO. *Sled Run.* Vol 80. Fiction.
FRED MISURELLA. *Only Sons.* Vol 79. Fiction.
FRANK LENTRICCHIA. *The Portable Lentricchia.* Vol 78. Fiction.
RICHARD VETERE. *The Other Colors in a Snow Storm.* Vol 77. Poetry.
GARIBALDI LAPOLLA. *Fire in the Flesh.* Vol 76 Fiction & Criticism.
GEORGE GUIDA. *The Pope Stories.* Vol 75 Prose.
ROBERT VISCUSI. *Ellis Island.* Vol 74. Poetry.
ELENA GIANINI BELOTTI. *The Bitter Taste of Strangers Bread.* Vol 73. Fiction.
PINO APRILE. *Terroni.* Vol 72. Italian Studies.
EMANUEL DI PASQUALE. *Harvest.* Vol 71. Poetry.
ROBERT ZWEIG. *Return to Naples.* Vol 70. Memoir.
AIROS & CAPPELLI. *Guido.* Vol 69. Italian/American Studies.
FRED GARDAPHÉ. *Moustache Pete is Dead! Long Live Moustache Pete!.* Vol 67. Literature/Oral History.
PAOLO RUFFILLI. *Dark Room/Camera oscura.* Vol 66. Poetry.
HELEN BAROLINI. *Crossing the Alps.* Vol 65. Fiction.
COSMO FERRARA. *Profiles of Italian Americans.* Vol 64. Italian Americana.
GIL FAGIANI. *Chianti in Connecticut.* Vol 63. Poetry.
BASSETTI & D'ACQUINO. *Italic Lessons.* Vol 62. Italian/American Studies.
CAVALIERI & PASCARELLI, Eds. *The Poet's Cookbook.* Vol 61. Poetry/Recipes.
EMANUEL DI PASQUALE. *Siciliana.* Vol 60. Poetry.
NATALIA COSTA, Ed. *Bufalini.* Vol 59. Poetry.
RICHARD VETERE. *Baroque.* Vol 58. Fiction.
LEWIS TURCO. *La Famiglia/The Family.* Vol 57. Memoir.
NICK JAMES MILETI. *The Unscrupulous.* Vol 56. Humanities.

BASSETTI. ACCOLLA. D'AQUINO. *Italici: An Encounter with Piero Bassetti.*
    Vol 55. Italian Studies.
GIOSE RIMANELLI. *The Three-legged One.* Vol 54. Fiction.
CHARLES KLOPP. *Bele Antiche Stòrie.* Vol 53. Criticism.
JOSEPH RICAPITO. *Second Wave.* Vol 52. Poetry.
GARY MORMINO. *Italians in Florida.* Vol 51. History.
GIANFRANCO ANGELUCCI. *Federico F.* Vol 50. Fiction.
ANTHONY VALERIO. *The Little Sailor.* Vol 49. Memoir.
ROSS TALARICO. *The Reptilian Interludes.* Vol 48. Poetry.
RACHEL GUIDO DE VRIES. *Teeny Tiny Tino's Fishing Story.*
    Vol 47. Children's Literature.
EMANUEL DI PASQUALE. *Writing Anew.* Vol 46. Poetry.
MARIA FAMÀ. *Looking For Cover.* Vol 45. Poetry.
ANTHONY VALERIO. *Toni Cade Bambara's One Sicilian Night.* Vol 44. Poetry.
EMANUEL CARNEVALI. *Furnished Rooms.* Vol 43. Poetry.
BRENT ADKINS. et al., Ed. *Shifting Borders. Negotiating Places.*
    Vol 42. Conference.
GEORGE GUIDA. *Low Italian.* Vol 41. Poetry.
GARDAPHÈ, GIORDANO, TAMBURRI. *Introducing Italian Americana.*
    Vol 40. Italian/American Studies.
DANIELA GIOSEFFI. *Blood Autumn/Autunno di sangue.* Vol 39. Poetry.
FRED MISURELLA. *Lies to Live By.* Vol 38. Stories.
STEVEN BELLUSCIO. *Constructing a Bibliography.* Vol 37. Italian Americana.
ANTHONY JULIAN TAMBURRI, Ed. *Italian Cultural Studies 2002.*
    Vol 36. Essays.
BEA TUSIANI. *con amore.* Vol 35. Memoir.
FLAVIA BRIZIO-SKOV, Ed. *Reconstructing Societies in the Aftermath of War.*
    Vol 34. History.
TAMBURRI. et al., Eds. *Italian Cultural Studies 2001.* Vol 33. Essays.
ELIZABETH G. MESSINA, Ed. *In Our Own Voices.*
    Vol 32. Italian/American Studies.
STANISLAO G. PUGLIESE. *Desperate Inscriptions.* Vol 31. History.
HOSTERT & TAMBURRI, Eds. *Screening Ethnicity.*
    Vol 30. Italian/American Culture.
G. PARATI & B. LAWTON, Eds. *Italian Cultural Studies.* Vol 29. Essays.
HELEN BAROLINI. *More Italian Hours.* Vol 28. Fiction.
FRANCO NASI, Ed. *Intorno alla Via Emilia.* Vol 27. Culture.
ARTHUR L. CLEMENTS. *The Book of Madness & Love.* Vol 26. Poetry.
JOHN CASEY, et al. *Imagining Humanity.* Vol 25. Interdisciplinary Studies.
ROBERT LIMA. *Sardinia/Sardegna.* Vol 24. Poetry.
DANIELA GIOSEFFI. *Going On.* Vol 23. Poetry.
ROSS TALARICO. *The Journey Home.* Vol 22. Poetry.
EMANUEL DI PASQUALE. *The Silver Lake Love Poems.* Vol 21. Poetry.
JOSEPH TUSIANI. *Ethnicity.* Vol 20. Poetry.
JENNIFER LAGIER. *Second Class Citizen.* Vol 19. Poetry.
FELIX STEFANILE. *The Country of Absence.* Vol 18. Poetry.

PHILIP CANNISTRARO. *Blackshirts*. Vol 17. History.
LUIGI RUSTICHELLI, Ed. *Seminario sul racconto*. Vol 16. Narrative.
LEWIS TURCO. *Shaking the Family Tree*. Vol 15. Memoirs.
LUIGI RUSTICHELLI, Ed. *Seminario sulla drammaturgia*.
   Vol 14. Theater/Essays.
FRED GARDAPHÈ. *Moustache Pete is Dead! Long Live Moustache Pete!*.
   Vol 13. Oral Literature.
JONE GAILLARD CORSI. *Il libretto d'autore. 1860 - 1930*. Vol 12. Criticism.
HELEN BAROLINI. *Chiaroscuro: Essays of Identity*. Vol 11. Essays.
PICARAZZI & FEINSTEIN, Eds. *An African Harlequin in Milan*.
   Vol 10. Theater/Essays.
JOSEPH RICAPITO. *Florentine Streets & Other Poems*. Vol 9. Poetry.
FRED MISURELLA. *Short Time*. Vol 8. Novella.
NED CONDINI. *Quartettsatz*. Vol 7. Poetry.
ANTHONY JULIAN TAMBURRI, Ed. *Fuori: Essays by Italian/American Lesbiansand Gays*. Vol 6. Essays.
ANTONIO GRAMSCI. P. Verdicchio. Trans. & Intro. *The Southern Question*.
   Vol 5. Social Criticism.
DANIELA GIOSEFFI. *Word Wounds & Water Flowers*. Vol 4. Poetry. $8
WILEY FEINSTEIN. *Humility's Deceit: Calvino Reading Ariosto Reading Calvino*.
   Vol 3. Criticism.
PAOLO A. GIORDANO, Ed. *Joseph Tusiani: Poet. Translator. Humanist*.
   Vol 2. Criticism.
ROBERT VISCUSI. *Oration Upon the Most Recent Death of Christopher Columbus*.
   Vol 1. Poetry.

www.ingramcontent.com/pod-product-compliance
Lightning Source LLC
Chambersburg PA
CBHW030050100426
42734CB00038B/989